WRINKLES DON'T HURT

By
Carol Hersh

PublishAmerica
Baltimore

Hardcover 9781462670789
PUBLISHED BY PUBLISHAMERICA, LLLP
www.publishamerica.com
Baltimore

Printed in the United States of America

This book is dedicated to all baby boomers who are having trouble keeping up with technology.

WRINKLES DON'T HURT

This is a hilarious story
about two baby boomers,
Lola Able and James Cain,
who were born in the 40's,
went to school in the 50's,
grew up in the 60's,
and got married in the 70's.

When Johnny comes marching home again hoorah, hoorah!

In the 40's, the boys came home. Babies were booming. That is where the title baby boomers comes from.

Take this test to see if you are a baby boomer. Can you name five of the Little Rascals? If you do not know who the Little Rascals are, then you are not a baby boomer.

A wholesome time

It was a wholesome time to grow up. We played games like tag, cops and robbers, and hopscotch. The first TV that came out was black and white with a screen in front of it to magnify the picture. We watched shows like *Rin Tin Tin, Lassie*, and *Chief Halftown*. Western's , lots and lots of westerns, and of course, of course, a horse, the famous *Mr. ED*! "Hey gang, what time is it? *It's Howdy Doody Time!*" Then there was a man named Walt, who started a club about a mouse. We all remember two of the first members, Annette and Cubby! I can even remember what time the Mickey Mouse club came on. I had to eat dinner every night at five o'clock with Mickey, and the Club, and my cat, who ate all my green vegetables. (mom and dad never knew).

Back then there was even a dolfin, named *Flipper,* that was so smart. The sitcoms always had a mature neighbor down the street. *Dennis the Menace* was always yelling, "Mr. WILSON". Then I got the most depressing thought, Oh my gosh, now I'm that mature person who lives down the street.

The hula-hoop takes its place in history, here. Do you remember the first kid on your block to get one? Back in those days, life was so simple. We had Good Old-Fashioned Simple Fun! No cell phones, no computers, no buttons to push .

In the 50's, the most complicated device was the party line. You had to wait for your neighbors to get off the phone, before making your call. You could actually listen in on their conversation. I mentioned this to a younger person, and she said, "What if you had an emergency?" I said "didn't you ever hear of a busy signal?" Then I remembered, she probably had call waiting, and there was no such thing as a busy signal. Then I realized. Oh my gosh, I am writing a history book!

There was no need to be concerned about kids getting too fat. We rode bikes, and roller-skated. There was no sitting in front of a TV, or computer to play games all day.

Sex, drugs and rock and roll

Then in the 60s, the Pepsi generation was coming at us, and going strong. We burned bras, and tie-dyed everything. Miniskirts were the new fashion statement. Bell-bottoms came in and the gays came out. We ended that decade with Woodstock, something that will never be forgotten. We knew how to make our mark in history. What good music we had!

A time of maturity.

Lola graduated from college and became a stewardess. In those days, they were called "stewardess", and they were all females.

Then in the 70's, Lola and James decided to get married. The papers had fun with their names. The headlines read, "Cain marries Able" on April 1. It was a hippie wedding, no invitations, gowns, or music. It was an outdoor ceremony ,on a mountain top at sun set ,in a bad thunderstorm. A small crowd had gathered, in the storm, to wait for the bride, and groom. Lola and James were a half hour late, and the Minister expected a messenger to show up with a note saying. *"April fools," Lola and James.* For Lola and James, growing up was over; it was down to business, now. However, James and Lola were not ready to grow up and leave the college way of life. They packed there skis in their VW camper and headed for the Rockies. Summertime came and they went to the beach, and got jobs as a waitres and a bartender. They did all that without a cell phone. Amazing, isn't it?

Bigger is not always better

Back in the 40's and 50's, 78rpm records were popular. Lola remembers her first album by Elvis Presley. When she had a nice collection of 78 albums, they came out with the smaller 45 records.

So she started collecting 45's . Not long after that, they came out with a small eight-track tape. Eventually, the even smaller, cassettes, became popular. Each time technology changed, we had to change our way of enjoying our favorite music. The CD came out with new machines to play the new song's. This was very convenient to store and to play in our cars. Likewise, we went from the big boom - box to a smaller transistor and then even smaller IPOD. Progress is nice but very expensive.

The same thing happened to the telephone...small,smaller smallest!

Now you could take pictures and send e-mail on your phone. Wow! The baby boomers had to keep up with the times. Technology kept changing things. It was like being back in school; every night Lola would go to bed with an instruction booklet. She had a very hard time learning these new little contraptions. However, her little daughter had no problem at all. One tine while traveling, she took her daughter to her grandparents, with a VCR, to help them baby-sit her. They had a hard time understanding the VCR. .Lola's daughter, who could not read yet, told them how to turn it on and play. She knew where the buttons were to push. They could not believe, that a one year old, was teaching them how to run a VCR!

All of a sudden, life was not so simple anymore. However, we could carry our phone in our pocket as well as our music. No more, boom boxes .The same thing was happening with the cameras. They kept getting smaller. My 35-millimeter camera, with its different size lenses, was becoming obsolete. I did not find the new digital cameras easier. I t was much smaller than a 35mm. However, the prices were getting smaller too.

It is amazing, but the same thing happened with computers. The first one was humongous. Now they are so small. You can put one in your brief case. Amazing!

Flying the Friendly Skies

After college, Lola became a stewardess. She exhausted her banking account by buying discounted tickets. Her and her roommate Jane, bought a $60 round-trip ticket to London. Lola bought a new volkswagon in the states, and picked it up at the factory in Bremin, Germany. A little man in a white coat, delivered it to her at the factory. While all the factory workers gathered round to look at it. They wanted to look at a car designed for the states. It was safe back then, for a girl to travel around. There were youth hostles in Europe, where you could stay cheaply . After a few weeks of traveling with Jane, they got tired of not being able to talk to anyone else. Jane was the only English speaking person she knew there. They decided to pick up a hitchhicker, a cute French soldier, now they would have someone different to talk to. Never thinking he couldn't talk to them anyway,they drew pictures to communicate. After a while, they needed a bathroom. When in the pub, Lola asked the soldier where the ladies room was. He directed her to the door. When she opened the door it was a closet with a drain in the floor. She chuckled, thinking he directed her to the mens room. Went outside and asked him where the ladies room was. He laughed, indicating they were the same. Back in she went wondering how she was going to accomplish this task having slacks and pants on. "How strange."

The soldier friend took them home to his house to spend the night, but his mother wanted nothing to do with two

American girls. So he took them across the street to Peire's house, who spoke English. His father had a travel trailer where they were able to spend the night. While at pierrs they were treated very nicely. Peire was impressed when his father opened a can of cherries, he said we only eat these on special occasions. They settled down in the travel trailer bed when there was a knock at the door. In came the little hunched French man and said "avez vous chaud". Jane and Lola knew exactly what he said but pretended not undertand. After several rounds of no comprendez, he finally left. They were not going to let him in their bed. The next morning they split at five am, before anyone was up, for Paris.

Facing reality
One-day friends showed up at the beach, with a truck and said, "We are taking you home, and you are going to get real jobs." Therefore, it was.

Lola became a very successful business woman. She developed Multiple Sclerosis, and had to quit her business, which is where the wheels come in, due to it eventually leaving her in a wheelchair?

Lola always had a good attitude. She

knew she was going to handle her handicap. She looked at it as being in a bad storm, and she knew she would whether the weather, whatever the weather, whether see liked the weather or not.

Lola keeps rolling along, staying positive and keeping her chin up high.

Before the ADA

Before the Americans with disabilities act, there were no curb cuts, or handicapped parking spaces. Lola kept weathering the weather with that good old Pepsi generation feeling. It did get a little easier for the handicapped, after the ADA. No one understood that accessible meant flat. She still would be banging into the curb cut trying to get over it. One time, a man stopped at a red light, watched her bang into the curb several times before he got out of his car and lifted her front wheel over the curb. The curb cut was just too high, preventing her from getting up onto the sidewalk.

Lola found people, always willing to help.

She was not used to this compassion. One time, while using a cane, she really wanted to buy some fresh rolls at the bakery. When her turn came, there were none left.. The next batch would not be done for 10 minutes. She told the clerk she could not stand that long, therefore, she would be waiting in her car. In 10 minutes, someone was knocking on her car door with a bag of rolls . Lola could not believe the kindness of this stranger. As she searched her purse for the money, she had overwhelming tears in her eyes.'

The ADA was trying by making accessibility mandatory. Somehow, retail establishments just could not get it. One place she frequented, put the handicap stall in the women's room, the furthest from the door. She got into it, but could not get out of it because the sinks were 2 feet from it. She did not have enough room to turn the wheelchair. Another place, very nicely installed a handicapped pushbutton, but every week had a chair in front of it, preventing you to get close enough to push it. Her service dog could not even get close enough. She just could not understand why other people could not understand the handicap's challenge! They would make it easy for them, but then prevent them from using it. What has happened to common sense?

Break a leg!

Lola slipped off her commode ,the fall was around a foot, but she could not move her leg since she was sitting on them. Thinking nothing was wrong she went into bed, but the next morning her aide said we are going to the hospital "your leg is broken". She could not believe a simple slip could end up a fracture. She thought a fracture would be corrected with a cast and off she would go," Wrong" it required an operation, bars, five screws and a plate and bone grafting and her tibia was fixed. The doctor says "but I did it". She was wondering why he had any doubt. Hello osteoporosis.

Lola traveles around her room in a ceilling

lift to get in bed and in to her hair. One day her aide did not have the hoyer pad on right and Lola slipped out on the floor breaking her femur. Same thing all over again: bars, screws, plates and five day hospital stay. She now gets treated with a daily injection for osteoporosis

Early sings of MS

While skiing in the French Alps with her friends, which she always kept up with, she noticed she couldn't keep up with them anymore. So the next morning she decided she would take a lesson. She chose the advanced class but what she had not figured was the instructer would speak French. Therfore, she didn't learn a thing and could not keep up. Skiing back to the lodge deck, she was sitting in the sun enjoying a glass of wine. All around her were the French drinking there Peirre, and sunning their v-necks. All of a sudden, someone came up to her and said "What part of the states are you from?" Lola said, "How do you know

I am an American? I look like everybody else." He said, "You have scott goggles on, no one in Europe wears them." Then she realized the streachy band around her head said scott giving her away as an American. She chatted with the bus boy named Gary. They were both happy to find someone that spoke English. That night back in her chalet with her friends, they were enjoying a meal prepared by their chalet cheft. And of all a sudden, the sliding glass door on the second floor opens and Gary appears. He introduces himself. "Hi, I'm Gary from California." She had no idea how he found her!

She just wasn't skiing right that week, because after you got off the cable car, to get to the slope, you had to walk down, 60 steps in your ski boots while carrying your skis and poles. She could not handle the steps, this was very disturbing. She did not know what was happening, and it was scary.

Wrinkles do not hurt

Now, let us deal with wrinkles. Since all the baby boomers, which was the majority of the population, were wrinkling. There were many anti-wrinkling products! There was always hope that some day, someone would get it right. Until then, just get over it! *Wrinkles do not hurt.*

One time Lola was with her two year old daughter, Shelly, at a doctors office. Shelley asked a very mature woman in a wheelchair "do you hurt" and the woman answered "no. Why do you ask? " She replied, "don't all those lines in your face hurt?" The woman laughed and said, "No honey, if you are lucky, and live a long life as I have, you might be lucky enough to have them too. They are called laugh lines"

Lola did not have any gray hair, but that is not a problem. Is it? James had a whole head of gray hair with a tiny sparse spot on the top of his head. He was so tall that you only could see it when he sat down. Lola found his hair, though, under her chin! Wrinkles were no problem for men. They just made them look more distinguished and sexy. He still had a great bode and announced he was not ready to stop living, referring to Lola's, wheels. James could not handle the weather though. Therefore, he took off. See James run, see James run, right into the arms of a 20 year younger woman.

Lola just kept rolling on! One day at the supermarket, she was rolling down aisle two. See Lola roll, see Lola roll right into the mustard at the end of the aisle. She just could not cut the mustard right, and oops! There went the whole display. Cleanup at the end of aisle two!

Lola and her 10-year-old daughter went to the movies. She parked her scooter in the aisle and transferred to the end seat next to her daughter. When the movie was over, she transferred back to her scooter, before the lights came on, so she could leave before the multitudes got up. It was still very dark and she did not notice her purse strap was over the controls, depressing the speed ·

switch. So when she turned the key on, the scooter went full speed ahead. Luckily, no one had got up yet, so the aisle was empty. She could not imagine, what was wrong, because it was so dark. She could not find the switch to solve that. Therefore, before she knew what was happening, she went right into the front wall, where the screen is! The theater became very quiet, all eyes were looking at the crazy woman who ran her scooter into the front wall. She turned around and smiled to her friend sitting with her daughter. The friend then said, "She is all right!" Lola went back to her daughter, saying, "It was so dark I couldn't see the control." Her daughter said, "Why didn't you turn the key off?" Duh! Did not think of that.

Let's talk

What was it like to be handicapped in the 80s? Right from the point of diagnosis Lola realized she was the only person in charge of her body, and only she knew, what was happening in her body. Not much was known about M. S., in the 80s. She trusted her doctor, but at the same time, Lola realized she knew her own body. He knew everything that the books said, but at the same time, it was *her disease*. She was aggressive with drugs from the beginning. She tried all the alternative medicines she then had experimental chemo treatments in the hospital. Lola was not on the cancer floor, so the nurses were not familiar with the drug. Signs were posted all over her door for the nurses' safety: *When entering room, wear gloves.* It was so funny when a little deliveryman came to bring flowers, saw the signs and was a bit scared to come in. He put the flowers down quickly, turned around, and went through the closest door. Lola was laughing inside, because she knew it was her bathroom door! He came back out feeling embarrassed and quickly left the room.

Bald is beautiful

Lola made the most of being bald. Actually, she enjoyed it. How many people know what their whole skull looks like? Lola thought hers was quite pretty. Back in the 80's, it was strange to see a bald headed woman. Nowadays it is quite common. One day, Lola was sitting in the passenger's seat of her car in front of the 711 waiting for James. A man, on the phone, saw her sitting in the car wearing a hat, since it was winter. Therefore, she looked normal. He turned his back, and Lola got rather warm in the car and took her hat off. When he was finished with his call, he turned around and was flabbergasted to see a bald woman in the car. She loved shocking people! Her daughter did too. After all, being one, she just grew hair. James, Lola and Shelly, were sitting in a busy restaurant, having a nice dinner, Being winter, Lola was wearing a hat, when all of a sudden, Shelly decides to take Lola's hat off! Shelly had the trickiest smile on her face and thought this was so funny. It was funny, but Lola did not appreciate it. It was the only time Lola felt embarrassed being bald.

The diagnosis of Multiple Sclerosis required her to spend a good amount of time doing exercises. Lola faithfully went to a yoga class, and enjoyed swimming laps at the gym. Having faith in God that she will walk again, she wanted to keep her body ready. She even used *walk again*, as her e-mail address. Always being positive, and always reading about what was happening with MS.

Living on a limited Income

When Lola was diagnosed, she was put on Social Security. Her long and steady work history deemed her eligible.

She is still trying to adjust to this, but considers herself lucky that the government will watch after her. Medicare also is a blessing. It covers her many doctors bills. Without Social Security and Medicare, she would not be able to do it alone. Lola had a long, fun life before becoming disabled. She is content to sit in her garden, watching her koi fish swim. She realizes many people become disabled before they really have had a chance to live. She is glad she did every thing, while she was young. Even though she and James, went into debt a lot to do it. If she waited for retirement, it would have been too late.

Traveling

Europe was not ready for Lola. She did not think they left the handicapped, out of the house, because they have steps everywhere. Even the dogs followed her scooter down the street, looking at it strangely. Lola and James stayed in a hotel in Paris having steps to exit from the lobby to the street. James needed assistance getting Lola's scooter out of the hotel. Two bellhops were at the bottom of the steps. Not knowing French, James tried to ask for assistance with the scooter by putting his right hand on his left bicep and placing his left hand on his left shoulder. The bellhops were looking at him very strangely. He did this several times, trying to indicate he needed muscle power. Lola just looked at him in disbelief, while the two young bellhops had an awful expression on their face. They were wondering what this crazy American was trying to say. Lola said, "James, don't you know, that means something else in America? " Realizing what he was doing, he quickly ran down to the bellhops and explained what he was trying to say. They looked relieved.

Lola speaks

So often people are asking me, what is it like to be handicapped? So I thought I would think about it, and put it in writing. Its been a long gradual process of losing your bodies capabilities But looking on the brighter side, it has given me a lot of time to do things that I would not have done. Like reading , and studying the Bible. I take time now to smell the roses. I miss being able to work in my garden myself, others must do it for me. And believe it or not, I miss being able to clean my own house! So see it is not that bad. Some people say, "What do you do with all your time? ' There really isn't a lot of time. With exercising, therapy and Dr. appointments, I really only have two hours a day to myself. Aides come in the morning, and in the evening. Putting me in and getting me out of bed ,takes a rather long time. I can't do anything that involves my feet or legs. My hands are limited, they have trouble with the phone and light switches, which leaves knitting and crocheting out of the picture.

It's the simple things in life, that mean so much. I have Meals on Wheels, and during the holidays, they use volunteers to deliver the meals. One Thanksgiving a mother brought her four children to deliver my meal. I was in bed when they appeared, lining themselves up on my ramp smallest to tallest. The smallest boy brought me a turkey made of Popsicle sticks, and explained it was a magnet for the refrigerator. The next child gave me a card explaining whom they represented. By this time, my eyes were overcome with tears, and I could not read the card. I could not imagine that I was in this position to need this, and someone would do this for me. It was such a moving moment. I still have the turkey on my refrigerator.

I hope this will answer some of your questions. I hope it might have helped someone too.

This brings us to the conclusion of the story; the last chapter is a fairy tale because the baby boomers are still with us.

Answer to the baby boomer quiz:

Five little rascals: Alfalfa, Buckwheat, Darla, Froggy, and Spanky.

The future is now

Lola moved into a senior high-rise with a view of the ocean. She was very happy there. There was a coffee shop at the corner, and Lola and her friends would meet and ride down to the corner.

Lola was the leader of the group. She arranged for the group to have free coffee on Mondays. A whole line of chairs wheeled down the block. Passers-by honked their horns at them, and they honked back!

They would be singing songs. Some days, when the sun was not out, they would sing, *"The Sun Will Be Out Tomorrow"*, other days they would sing *"What a Friend We Have in Jesus"*.

They were known as" The Holy Rollers". It was an outdoor café, and some stayed for lunch.

Lola had a rule, no complaining, or mention of aches or pains.

When returning home, they would play games. They were a Happy Bunch"!

She lived out her life on wheels, next to the ocean, watching the waves roll in and out; just what she always wanted for the future.

She lived the rest of her life happily ever after.

This is the end of the fairytale.

I hope you enjoyed my book.

Bless You

Don't Worry... BE Happy!

Less Wrinkles

CPSIA information can be obtained at www.ICGtesting.com
Printed in the USA
BVOW041825200612

292850BV00001BD/1/P